Swim Your Best

Be the Athlete You Want To Be

Jeremy Boone

ISBN-13:
978-0615726236 (Athlete By Design Press)

ISBN-10:
0615726232

Published by:

This journal is available in higher quantities and group/team discounts. For more information please visit www.athletebydesign.com.

Additional Resources and Seminars by Jeremy Boone

Ready To Play Mental Profile

Play Your Best

Get Faster Now

Lower Body Performance for Sport

Coach Your Best

Parent Your Best

Building a House of Champions

You can find Jeremy online at the following websites

www.athletebydesign.com

http://www.parentyourbest.com/

www.coachyourbest.com

Be the Athlete You Want To Be

This journal is dedicated to my mother Patsy Boone who lost her life to breast cancer in 2000 at the early age of 52.

She always encouraged me to discover the best version of me and share it with the world. I hope the information in this journal will help you to do the same in both sports and in life.

Contents

Introduction

Jeremy Boone

"Working on the inside shows on the outside."- G. Mack

Growing up as a young athlete, one of my favorite coaches always used to say *"Win or lose, playing sports can be one of life's greatest experiences or one of life's most frustrating experiences, it's your choice."* There is nothing like being part of a team that survives grueling practices in the pool, escapes a near loss during a season, finds ways to win meets when you are the underdog, and all for a chance to win a championship while having fun. And yet while this journey may be a dream for most athletes and a reality only for a few, there is something even better that comes from playing sports. Win or lose, your journey as an athlete will challenge you to discover the best version of you, and if that happens, no one or nothing can stop you.

So what does the best version of you as an athlete look like?

That's exactly what this journal is going to help you find out! This journal is for you if:

- You want a competitive edge
- You have a goal of making it to the next level
- You want to make swimming a lifelong sport

- You want to make right now count the most
- You have a desire to be your best
- You want to get the most out of your swimming experience
- You want to have more fun in your sport

Imagine if fun never left the pool by the time you were a senior in high school. Imagine if you had a team made up of your coaches, parents, and teammates that kept your passion for swimming alive rather than burning out, practices that were engaging rather than boring, and performances that were fulfilling rather than simply good or bad.

Your athletic journey is about what YOU want and the exercises and tools in this journal will help you to become the kind of athlete that you want to be and build a support team to help you get there.

Where did this journal come from?

This journal is a summation of all of the wonderful conversations I have had with athletes, coaches, and parents since 1994 in an effort to help them be their best. This includes working with young athletes and their families as young as age six, all the way to working with Olympians and professional athletes in the NFL, NBA, NASCAR, PGA, MLB, English Premier League, NSCAA, swimming, tennis, and others.

It is by no means an all inclusive resource, as there is just way too much material to write in a single training journal or book. Instead, it is meant to be a catalyst for you to begin to think about the best version of you. It is meant to be used as a catalyst for meaningful conversations with those who influence you the most such as your parents, coaches, and teammates. Why? **Because the healthier your relationships are with those who mean the most to you, the better you will perform in the pool!**

There have been numerous athletes just like you that have used this material and accepted the challenge of becoming the best version of themselves. I want for you to be able to share their same story of celebration and make it yours.

Thanks for letting me be a part of your team!

J. Boone

How To Get The Most Out Of This Journal

Think of the Swim Your Best Training Journal™ (aka the SYBTJ) as your own personal coach, using it to help you learn more about yourself, discover your own strengths and weaknesses, and how to put yourself in a position to consistently perform your best.

In this twelve step program you are encouraged to work through each chapter with another teammate, your coach, a small group, or your entire team. It is suggested that you meet once or twice per week and cover only one chapter per session. Most athletes choose to meet right before or after practice. The format choice is whatever works best for you and allows you to take your time working through all of the exercises.

Why a journal is better than a book

A journal can be one of the most important tools in your equipment bag as an athlete. If you have never used a journal before, here are some of the main benefits of how using the SYBTJ can help you be your best as well as give you a competitive advantage at the next level:

- It creates self-awareness and encourages self-reflection of your past experiences
- It can allow you to take a different perspective or vantage point when making key decisions
- It can help address any problems or mental errors you might be dealing with
- It creates accountability with yourself in your efforts to achieve your desired results

- It can help you create clarity in your thinking
- It can serve as a tool to help you better communicate with others (family, coaches, teammates, etc)
- It can create a blueprint for your successes so you can give yourself the best chance to repeat them in the future

The SYBTJ is divided up into two sections. The first section will walk you through the seven key qualities of athletic excellence. You will be challenged to work through each of these qualities as it applies to your own life personally and as an athlete.

The second section will take you through the four key stages of what it takes to become your best.

This unique framework is based on the stages of human growth created by Dr. Robert S. Hartman and my good friend Dr. David Mefford, and comes from a little known science called *Sports Axiology*, the science of decision making and values in sport.

In each stage you will be asked to complete various questions and exercises designed to increase your self-awareness, give you more confidence as an athlete, and create an unshakable sense of self-esteem no matter how well you perform.

You can't become great on your own

No great athlete has achieved greatness on their own. They have all had someone else help them along their path to greatness. Therefore, all throughout section two of the SYBTJ, you will find checkboxes along with a space for the initials of either your coach, your parents, or an accountability partner indicating you have completed that particular exercise or critical conversation.

An accountability partner is someone who you trust that will not judge you, but instead help hold your feet to the fire and celebrate with you in the end. This can be a teammate, a coach, or just a friend. It's your choice!

In fact, before you get started, go ahead and write down the name of who you want your accountability partner to be:

_____

Accountability Partner Name

Now, I want you to get their signature below! Let them know that you have decided to take a more serious approach to being your best, and that you would like for them to help you along your journey.

I, _____ (their name), am willing to be an accountability partner with _____ (your name). I understand that my role includes being supportive not judging, challenging not correcting, and encouraging not discouraging in helping him/her becoming their best.

_____

Accountability Partner Signature

If you let it, the Swim Your Best Training Journal™ can have a huge impact on your athletic performance. Remember though, you will only get out of it as much as you are willing to put into it. So with a little extra effort and dedication to yourself, you can give yourself the best chance to play your winning game. It's worth it I promise!

If you ever have any questions or are looking for more specific help regarding your mental game visit www.athletebydesign.com.

Be the Athlete You Want To Be

Step #1: Discovering Your Self-Identity

"Whether you believe you can or you can't you are right."- Henry Ford

Do you consider yourself to be an athlete? One of the foundational principles of human performance is that you cannot outperform your own self-identity. What you believe about yourself as an athlete and as a person has a direct impact on your ability to consistently perform your best.

Your self-identity is how you see yourself. It is about who you are, what you do, and who you want to become. It is this quality alone that is the greatest determiner of your journey of athletic success and directly impacts all other mental qualities. Athletes who struggle with self-confidence, mental toughness, self-motivation, focus, etc. almost always will also be struggling with their own self-identity and what they believe about themselves.

What is the overall quality of your current self-identity? Circle the number that best applies to you (1=low and 5=high)

As a person   1 2 3 4 5

As an athlete   1 2 3 4 5

Athlete's who have a strong self-identity feel like they belong in the sports world. They can't imagine what life would even be like without participating in sports at all! There is a strong sense of conviction that being an athlete is part of who they want to be.

What do you believe about yourself? List the top three qualities of what you like and dislike most about yourself both as a person and as an athlete.

Like as a person	Dislike as a person
1.	1.
2.	2.
3.	3.

Like as an athlete	Dislike as an athlete
1.	1.
2.	2.
3.	3.

How do each of your beliefs affect your ability to perform your best? Which ones are in your control and which ones are beyond your control?

Do you ever find yourself struggling with your own self-identity? If so, what happens to your performance?

Sometimes athlete's who struggle with a clear self-identity do so because they look to others to define who they are. This can be a coach, a parent, teammates, or even friends who are outside of your sport. Maybe they don't believe you have what it takes to be a good athlete, or on the flip side maybe they have a false sense that you are way better than you actually are.

Who do you let influence you in your own thoughts and beliefs about yourself as a person and as an athlete?

Are their opinions actually true? Do they even matter? If so, why do they matter to you and how does this impact your belief in yourself?

So what's the bottom line?

It's your sport. YOU get to choose how you see yourself in it and what matters most to you. YOU get to choose how good you want to be. YOU get to choose what you believe about yourself. YOU get to choose how you let the people around you influence your own self-identity.

But whatever you choose, make sure it's your choice and be intentional about it.

In the space below, write down what you want your self-identity as a person and as an athlete to look like. What type of person do you what to be? What kind of athlete do you want to be?

What excites you the most about being an athlete?

Wrapping up, what is the one thing that you learned about yourself from this chapter that can have the greatest impact in your life and in your performance?

Step #2: Are you Coachable?

"Don't let what you can't do, interfere with what you can do."
- John Wooden

How well do you take instruction from others? Being coachable is about your willingness to allow other individuals to help you improve your performance. This includes being able to handle constructive criticism, being open to follow directions, and being proactive by asking others to help you improve.

Who do you trust, respect, and believe in to coach you?

_____(write coaches name here)

What three things do you look for in a coach when it comes to helping you improve?

1.

2.

3.

Athletes who struggle with coachability look at other's advice as conditional. In other words, you may or may not accept the instructions being offered to you. Other reasons for not being coachable may include:

- Lack of clear communication between you and your coach
- Lack of respect/trust
- You just like doing things your own way

- You secretly want to be on another team or in another group
- You don't believe your coach has the ability to help you
- You don't like your coach as a person

Do any of these ring true for you? If so, what action step(s) are you going to take to address it?

How coachable are you? Circle the number that best applies to you (1=low and 5=high)

Open to receive advice in public   1 2 3 4 5

Open to receive advice in private   1 2 3 4 5

Ask others for help   1 2 3 4 5

Overall coachable attitude   1 2 3 4 5

Intentionally applying feedback   1 2 3 4 5
from your coach.

How do you think your coach would answer each of these about you?

Open to receive advice in public   1 2 3 4 5

Open to receive advice in private   1 2 3 4 5

Ask others for help   1 2 3 4 5

Overall coachable attitude   1 2 3 4 5

Intentionally applying feedback   1 2 3 4 5
from your coach.

Looking back at your own answers, if you circled any number less than five, what has to happen for that number to get to a five? What action steps are you willing to take to make that happen?

Sit down with your coach and make a list of the top three things that he/she believes you need to do to become a better athlete.

1.

2.

3

Ask your coach how you can be even more valuable to your team than you are right now. Describe your discussion below.

What would life be like for you if you were to commit to becoming even more coachable over the next thirty days?

Wrapping up, what is the one thing that you learned about yourself from this chapter that can have the greatest impact in your life and in your performance?

Step #3: Staying Focused

*"Obstacles are what you see when you take
your eyes off your goal." - Jim Lefebvre*

How well can you concentrate during your performance? Great athletes have the ability to focus on the task at hand and be able to eliminate distractions. This allows you to know what to do and when to do it when it comes to performing your best.

If I was attending one of your swim meets, how would I know that you are focused just by watching you? What are you doing? Who are you being?

List two recent events when you experienced laser-like focus. What was the outcome?

1.

2.

What allowed you to focus with precision and clarity?

How well do you currently focus in the following areas ? Circle the number that best applies to you (1=low and 5=high)

During practice   1 2 3 4 5

Before a meet   1 2 3 4 5

During a meet   1 2 3 4 5

Looking back at your own answers, if you circled any number less than five, what has to happen for that number to get to a five? What immediate action steps are you willing to take to make that happen?

Do you ever find that you focus better in one environment than another? (i.e. practice vs meet) If you focus better in practice than your meet is it due to the pressure that you feel or possibly pre- meet anxiety? Or do you find yourself getting too emotionally attached to the outcome of your meet before it even starts? If you focus better in your meet rather than practice is it because you feel like you only give your best effort when it counts? Write your answer below.

Become aware of when focusing is easy and when it is hard. If you struggle with focus it is likely because of the following reasons (though there are others these tend to be the main reasons of struggle):

1. Focus on things that are beyond your control
2. Can't let go of your mistakes and refocus on what matters most in the moment
3. You get easily distracted (both positive and negative)
4. You lack clarity in understanding what's being asked of you
5. You may feel discouraged
6. There may be a lack of trust between you and your teammates
7. You are disorganized in your race plan
8. You feel too much pressure to perform

List two events within the past week when you have struggled to focus the most. What was the reason for losing focus?

1.

2.

If you could hit the rewind button back to those moments, what would you have done differently? How would your focus have changed?

Here are some additional suggestions that will help improve your focus:

- Recognize when you begin to lose focus and ask yourself *'What matters most right now?'*
- Pre-meet visualization
- Controlled Breathing Patterns
- Self-talk
- Create a mistake ritual
- Establish a pre-meet ritual
- Learn to manage your emotions when things don't go your way

Wrapping up, what is the one thing that you learned about yourself from this chapter that can have the greatest impact in your life and in your performance?

Step #4: Mastering Self-Confidence

"The first and best victory is to conquer self."- Plato

Do you believe in yourself and your ability to achieve your goals? Self-confidence is about having a positive attitude and unshakable belief that you can perform your best.

How would you currently rate your own self-confidence in the following areas ? Circle the number that best applies to you (1=low and 5=high)

During practice   1 2 3 4 5

Before a meet   1 2 3 4 5

During a meet   1 2 3 4 5

Here are some truths about athletes who are self-confident:

- Understand the importance of having a positive attitude
- Able to separate who they are as a person from their performance
- Have a clear understanding of their own self-worth
- Believe in themselves no matter what
- Have faith in their ability to execute their race strategy
- Know that they will be a difference maker
- Are clear about their role and their ability to fulfill their role
- Feel that training and practice brings out their best
- Disagree that their performance has any major problems
- Love to work hard and prepare
- Are physically competent (in-shape and swim fit)
- Able to accept constructive criticism
- Will positively influence others (without even knowing it)

Which of the these statements best describes you when you feel the most self-confident? (pick three)

Athletes who tend to struggle with self-confidence can experience the following:

- Not clear about their role/position
- Lack of self-belief and trust in their own ability
- Agree that they have some personal/performance issues
- Struggle with consistently performing well
- May feel that no matter how hard the effort, it is still not enough
- Unhealthy relationship with coach/teammates/parents
- Rely on others to validate their own self-worth
- Have an emotional attachment to their results that serve to define their self-esteem and self-worth

Are there times when you struggle with any of these qualities that result in a lowering of your self-confidence? If so which one(s)? Why?

Here are some additional thoughts and questions on self-confidence.

What does performing your best and being fully confident look like? Who are you being? What are you doing?

What top three qualities do you bring to your performance when you swim your best?

    1.

    2.

    3.

What motivates you to practice and prepare to swim your best?

What has been your best performance ever in your sport? What were the things that you were able to control that contributed to being able to swim your best?

When you lack self-confidence how do you typically respond:

- Feelings:

- Thoughts:

- Actions:

What kind of self-talk, self-belief, and body language would you need to have to help turn your lack of self-confidence around in any moment?

Building self-confidence starts with who you are and what you do. If you are being hesitant, fearful, scared, or tentative that it will be hard to have self-confidence. List 3 things that you do that give you confidence by finishing the phrase '*I am good at....*'

1.

2.

3.

Write down three to five positive self-talk phrases that will help you regain your self-confidence when you struggle to swim your best.

Wrapping up, what is the one thing that you learned about yourself from this chapter that can have the greatest impact in your life and in your performance?

Step #5: Unrelenting Mental Toughness

"Under pressure you can perform fifteen percent better or worse." - Scott Hamilton

How do you define mental toughness? If you were to Google it online you would find there are over 90,000 websites that try and define it. In fact most coaches and athletes mistake mental toughness for plain toughness, but it is actually much more than that.

Mental toughness is simply your ability to endure the present in order to achieve your future goals and objectives.

There are two parts to being mentally tough. The first part is the word mental. In other words, how clear are you about what you are wanting to achieve as an athlete both now and long term? What is your purpose and vision of what you want to accomplish in your sport? If you lack clarity, then it is much more difficult to endure any present challenging or difficult situation.

The second part is about being tough and your attitude and willingness to never give up NO MATTER WHAT. It's about having the guts and never say die attitude during the most challenging of times so that you can endure the present.

How would you currently rate your own mental toughness in the following areas ? Circle the number that best applies to you (1=low and 5=high)

During practice   1 2 3 4 5

Before a meet   1 2 3 4 5

During a meet   1 2 3 4 5

Athletes who display mental toughness usually have the following qualities:

- A clear self-identity of who you are and who you want to become
- A strong self-belief in what you stand for
- A winning attitude no matter what the challenge or circumstances
- Are disciplined and committed to their efforts in all that they do
- Know how to handle mistakes and overcome failures
- Bring a proactive attitude when faced with roadblocks such as an injury or poor performance
- Show a relentless pursuit in their desire to improve

Which of the qualities above (or others) best represent you when you are mentally tough? (choose at least two)

Athletes who struggle with mental toughness experience the following:

- Lack clear goals and direction
- Will magnify mistakes
- Quit when things become challenging or difficult
- Use negative self-talk
- Show poor body language
- Lack discipline, motivation, and persistence
- Feel out of control
- Focus on the possibility of negative outcomes
- Lack clarity in their self-identity as a person and an athlete

When you find yourself struggling with mental toughness, which of these qualities best represent you?

So what's the secret to developing mental toughness? There is no secret! Here are the steps to what it takes to becoming more mentally tough:

1. Know yourself, your own strengths and weaknesses, and believe in yourself no matter what
2. Define a clear vision and purpose of what you want to accomplish in your sport and why this is important to you.
3. Challenge yourself at being uncomfortable everyday in order to develop toughness
4. Put your vision out in front everyday at practice and before your performances

Here are some additional thoughts, questions, and ideas about mental toughness.

Who is the most mentally tough athlete that you know?

What qualities do they have that make them mentally tough?

Describe a recent time when you were mentally tough. What was your biggest challenge that you had to overcome? What kept you from quitting? What was the outcome?

Describe a time when you chose to quite. What was your biggest challenge at that moment? Why did you choose to quit? What were you feeling? If you could go back and relive that moment what would you have done differently?

What has to happen in order for you to be able to 'turn on' your mental toughness switch?

What could you truly achieve if you committed your heart and mind to it?

How will you know that you have achieved your dreams and goals? Is it a feeling? Is it something tangible like winning an Olympic Medal or championship trophy? Is it something someone says to you? Is it a specific experience?

How do YOU want to celebrate your accomplishment? Who do you want to celebrate with?

What are you willing to give up to get there?

Wrapping up, what is the one thing that you learned about yourself from this chapter that can have the greatest impact in your life and in your performance?

Step #6: Developing Self-Discipline

"Motivation gets you going. Discipline keeps you going." –Jim Ryan

What is the one thing you need in order to accomplish your goals and have any kind of athletic success? It's the one thing that every great athlete possesses. In fact, this is the one part of the athletic equation that you cannot do without.

Self-discipline is about having will power. It is about making a conscious effort to decide that you will do whatever it takes to go after your goals. It is about your ability to control your thoughts, emotions, actions, and behaviors that could potentially distract you from achieving your goals and includes your ability to remain focused on the task at hand.

How would you currently rate your own self-discipline? Circle the number that best applies to you (1=low and 5=high)

Self-discipline   1   2   3   4   5

Athletes who are self-disciplined have the following qualities:

- Clear about what they want to achieve
- Remain focused and avoid distractions
- Established daily rituals and habits
- Realistic about what it will take to reach the goal
- Strong personal commitment and consistent effort
- Passionate and emotionally engaged
- Highly self-motivated
- Intentional and proactive in decision making
- Patiently persistent
- Make choices based on thinking rather than how they feel

- Use courage to overcome negative thoughts, feelings, emotions, and moods
- View self-discipline as an opportunity for freedom
- Understand that self-discipline is a skill and has to be developed
- Focus more on the process than their desired outcome
- Believes being self-disciplined allows for more fun not less
- Understands the importance of relaxation and recovery
- Constantly measures progress

Which of these statements best describe you when you practice self-discipline? Are there any statements that you wish described you but currently do not?

Most athletes who fall short of achieving their goals and dreams usually do so because they lack self-discipline and tend to experience the following:

- Have a strong fear of failure
- Get easily distracted
- Lack clarity in their purpose, vision, goals, objectives
- Driven by instant gratification and want immediate results
- Lack a daily routine
- Develop bad habits such as procrastination
- Struggle with emotional instability
- Let their feelings dictate decisions
- Tend to focus on what's easy versus what's best

- Believes self-discipline takes away fun
- Are impatient
- Focus more on the outcome than on the process

Do any of these statements currently describe you when you struggle with self-discipline? If so how does it make you feel? What could you accomplish as an athlete if you were more self-disciplined?

Here are some additional thoughts, questions, and ideas about self-discipline.

The greatest athletes understand that athletes develop daily not in a day.

Part of being self-disciplined means establishing good habits and a daily routine. What is your number one biggest time wasting habit?

If you were to get rid of this habit, how would it make you a better player? What would you be able to do more of and how would this impact your development?

How effective is your current daily training routine? Are there any gaps or areas that you can improve? (i.e. nutrition, stretching, etc.)

List two standards/expectations you have set for yourself when it comes to being the athlete that you want to be. How are you using self-discipline to reach those standards?

1.

2.

What would life be like for you if you were to commit to becoming even more self-disciplined over the next thirty days?

Wrapping up, what is the one thing that you learned about yourself from this chapter that can have the greatest impact in your life and in your performance?

Step #7: Improving Athletic Intelligence

"Some athletes have the ability to always win.
It's as though it's a natural state of mind."
-Sven-Goran Eriksson

What does it mean to be a smart swimmer? The more you know about the demands of swimming, the demands of each of the strokes, and your individual strengths and weaknesses, the better decisions you will be able to make under pressure.

Athletic intelligence is about how you use your knowledge and intuition to make good decisions that include the following:

1. How quickly and clearly you can make a decision

2. Your ability to cope under pressure and still make the best decision

3. How fast you can resolve a problem/situation

How would you rate your own athletic intelligence? Circle the number that best applies to you (1=low and 5=high)

Athletic Intelligence   1   2   3   4   5

In which of the three areas above do you feel are your strengths? Provide a recent example and describe the outcome.

Which of these same three areas do you feel you struggle with the most? Provide a recent example and describe the outcome.

Players who struggle with athletic intelligence typically do so because of the following:

- Lack of knowledge and understanding of their sport
- Struggle with timing of execution
- Lack true passion for swimming which leads to a decreased desire to learn and get better
- Tend to focus on the wrong things instead of what matters most in the moment
- Struggle with making decisions under pressure and feel rushed

Below is a simple framework for making great decisions that can help improve athletic intelligence. Adapt this framework into your training and practice by starting with simple drills and progress to more complex race scenarios.

1. **Read/Recognize**
   a. Knowledge of the situation
   b. Awareness of yourself
   c. Awareness of others
2. **React**
   a. Understand all of your options
   b. Make a good comparative choice that will give you the best result/outcome
3. **Respond**
   a. Execute and take action with confidence
   b. Proper timing

What are you doing to improve your current knowledge and understanding of the demands of your sport?

What are you doing to improve your current knowledge and understanding of the unique demands of each of your strokes?

Swimmers with high athletic intelligence have ALL three of the following qualities:

1. They understand the **purpose** of the technical aspects of each stroke and how this fits into the bigger picture of the overall race plan

2. They show **poise** in their ability to execute under pressure

3. They display a strong **passion** for playing the swimming

How about you? Do you also share these same three qualities? Would your coach agree?

Wrapping up, what is the one thing that you learned about yourself from this chapter that can have the greatest impact in your life and in your performance?

It's time to become GREAT

By now I hope you are starting to sharpen your mindset having worked through the first seven steps of Swim Your Best ™.

Which step did you enjoy the most and why?

Which step did you struggle with the most and why?

If the journal ended here, can you say you came closer to improving your mental game? How?

In truth, these steps are meant to prepare you for steps eight through twelve. Think of it like you have just finished your offseason and preseason Is about to begin. This is where things will really start to come together for you mentally. I hope you're ready!

The journey has just begun!

Step #8: Your Profile
-Know Yourself

"Knowing yourself is the beginning of all wisdom." -Aristotle

Have you ever taken the time to think about and write down an athletic description of yourself? What is it you want to achieve as an athlete this season? What do you want to achieve in the next few years? This step is all about understanding and becoming more aware of your own strengths and weaknesses, your desired goals and results, and those qualities that make you unique. Once you have laid it all out on the table, only then can you start to truly work on becoming the best version of you as an athlete.

Age-   Level-

Preferred Strokes (List the unique demands of each of your strokes)

  Physical (*i.e. strength, speed, power, agility, etc.*)

  Mental (*i.e. focus, mental toughness, etc*)

  Sports Skills (*i.e. hand/eye coordination, throwing, etc.*)

  Other (*i.e. team leader, being vocal, etc.*)

School/Club-

Coach-

Injury History-

Testing/Performance Evaluation Scores

Below enter in any offseason, preseason, or other performance testing results that you have completed. (i.e. fitness tests, strength & power tests, stroke counts, functional movement screen, etc.)

Date_____ Test_____ Score_____

Date_____ Test_____ Score_____

Date_____ Test_____ Score_____

Date_____ Test_____ Score_____

For specific examples of tests for competitive swimming performance and what some of the world's top swimmers do visit www.dmperformanceswimming.com.

Are you happy with your scores? Which ones do you need to improve upon most and why?

List below your PR Swim Times in each of your strokes/events:

What about swimming is important to you?

What about that (answer from above) is important to you?

List your top 3 strengths (can be physical, mental, or sports specific)

1.

2.

3.

What does performing with each of your top strengths look like ?

1.

2.

3.

List and describe your top 3 weaknesses (can be physical, mental, or sports specific)

1.

2.

3.

Pick the weakness that you believe will have the greatest negative impact on your performance and complete the following:

Weakness 1: *"I am willing to* _____

starting today to address this weakness."

"Improving this weakness will allow me to _____

_____ *so that*

_____. *"*

Weakness 2: *"I am willing to _____*

starting today to address this weakness."

"Improving this weakness will allow me to _____

_____*so that*

_____.*"*

Share your results with your accountability partner and describe your conversation below:

Accountability Partner Initials: _____

Sometimes not being able to swim your best has little to do with any roadblocks or weaknesses, but instead it may be more about what is missing from your performance.

What do you feel is missing from your performance right now? If you were to add or develop this, what would you be able to do differently?

1.

2.

3.

List an immediate one-step action plan to address each:

1.

2.

3.

Share your results with your accountability partner and describe your conversation below:

Accountability Partner Initials: _____

Now let's find out what some of your favorite things are about your sport.

Who is your favorite athlete in your sport?

Why is he/she your favorite athlete?

Who is your favorite college team in your sport and why?

List your top three favorite quote(s) as an athlete:

1.

2.

3.

Share with your accountability partner your favorite quotes and explain why they are your favorite. Did they have a favorite that you liked as well? Describe your conversation below.

Accountability Partner Initials: _____

Describe your best highlight as an athlete so far? What about this particular event/moment is most meaningful for you?

How do you want to be remembered by your teammates and coaches at the end of your season?

How do you want your opponents to describe you after a meet...win or lose?

Share your results with your accountability partner and describe your conversation below

Accountability Partner Initials: _____

Wrapping up, what is the one thing that you learned about yourself from this chapter that can have the greatest impact in your life and in your performance?

Okay, now that you have started to write down some different things to get to really know yourself better, it's time to get an opinion from others who have your best interest in mind. In the next section, you will be challenged to start thinking about building 'Team YOU'. In other words, who are all of the individuals in your life that can help you be the athlete that you want to be?

Step #9: Building Your Team
-Together I'll Swim Better

"Teamwork makes the dream work."- John Maxwell

What does the phrase *Together I'll Swim Better* mean to you? If you were to say this to your parents or to your coach, what would it mean? This quote is actually the theme for an event called *Building A House Of Champions™*. It is all about helping those individuals in your life understand that the healthier their relationship is with you, the better you will perform!

So who is on 'Team You'? How are each of these individuals helping you become your best? Is there anyone missing from your team right now?

List the members of Team You and the role that each plays in helping you achieve your desired results as an athlete. Finally, enter in a number 1-5 on how you feel the current quality of your relationship is with that person (1=poor and 5=great)

Sample list

Team Member	Role	R-Score
Head Coach		3
Trainer/Physical Therapy	Currently healthy	
Performance Coach	Improve strength	5
Mom and/or Dad	Support me	4
Skill Coach	Improve technique	4

Now create your own chart/database

Team Member	Role	R-Score

Team You- YOUR PARENTS

When it comes to your parents, their role should be seen as supportive and a partner in helping you develop your potential. One of the most important conversations that you can have with them is about celebration. Some athletes like for their parents to cheer loudly while others like for their parents to just watch and not stand-out.

Celebration can focus on your performance results, but it can also focus on other things such as improvement of a specific skill (i.e. starting out of the blocks, quality of your flip turns, number of strokes), consistency of your effort, quality of your decision making, etc.

Describe below what you want your parents to celebrate and how you want them to celebrate and praise you during your meets:

Now sit down with your parents and share with them what you wrote on the previous page. Describe your experience and the outcome of your conversation below:

Parent Initials: _____

Discuss with your parents what your expectations are of yourself and what their expectations are of you participating in your sport. It's important that this conversation happens even before your season if possible. That way, there can be no assumptions from either of you about each other at the end of the season which may lead to potential disappoint or frustration. Describe in as much detail as possible the outcome of your conversation below:

Parent Initials: _____

Have a conversation with your parents about the following statement and describe your experience below:

"Mom or Dad, when it comes to my sport, there are three things that I want you to know about me that you may not know..."

Parent Initials: _____

Team You- YOUR COACH

When it comes to your sport, your coach is one of the most influential people on your team! However, most athletes will rarely set aside time to meet with their coach and talk with them about their own performance. Instead, they just wait around for their coach to tell them what to do. Unfortunately this approach doesn't work in the long run. Why? Because coaching is all about a relationship!

Your coach can't give you their best unless you are willing to communicate with him or her. The more guessing your coach has to do about you, the worse it is for you!

Ask your coach the following and record answers:

Coach, what do you see are my top three strengths? How can I continue to improve in each of these?

    1.

    2.

    3.

Coach, what is the number one obstacle you see preventing me from swimming my best? What can I do to address this?

Have a conversation with your coach about the following statement and describe your experience below:

"Coach, when it comes to my sport, there are three things that I want you to know about me that you may not know."

Coach Initials: _____

Wrapping up, what is the one thing that you learned about yourself from this chapter that can have the greatest impact in your life and in your performance?

Now that you've had the opportunity to have some important conversations with a few key players on 'Team You', it's time to take the next step and begin to identify a few things about yourself that make you who you are.

Step #10: Best Version Of You
-Choose yourself

"Today you are you, that is truer than true. There is no one alive who is Youer than You." – Dr. Seuss

Do you ever compare yourself and your abilities to other teammates or your competition and wish you had their height, speed, strength, or skill? This step is all about choosing yourself and being confident in who you are and what you bring to your team and to your sport itself.

Accepting who you are (what makes you unique compared to any other athlete or person) and the talents that you have been given is an important step in becoming the best version of you. The problem comes when you find yourself focusing on what you don't have, those things that are beyond your own control such as height, body type, etc., or you adopt someone else's goals and aspirations as your own.

Imagine if you were to focus only on what YOU want to achieve and get from swimming? How great could you be if you were to give all of your attention to focusing on what makes you you?

List three things that you want to achieve this upcoming season

1.

2.

3.

Why are each of these results above important to you? (Be specific.)

1.

2.

3.

What are the action steps that it will take in order to achieve each of these results?

1.

2.

3.

Share your results with your accountability partner and describe your conversation below:

Accountability Partner Initials: _____

Your Values Drive the Process

In a survey of over 3,000 high school athletes, 86% had not ever sat down with their family and written out their core values. Have you ever written down your top five personal core values? The qualities, standards, and principals that are most important to you? Your personal core values are important because they influence the decisions and choices that you make.

> **Values » Decisions » Actions » Results**

Examples of core values include hard work, commitment, trust, honesty, relationships, leadership, excellence, teamwork, respect, family, academics, accountability, etc...

List your top five personal core values and try to put a descriptive word in front of each one (i.e. patiently persistent):

1.

2.

3.

4.

5.

What do each of these values look like during practice and during a swim meet?

1.

2.

3.

4.

5.

Share your results with your accountability partner and describe your conversation below:

Accountability Partner Initials: _____

Now sit down with your family and discuss your family's core values when it comes to your sport. Are they different than your own? Write down your family's core values (include a descriptive word in front of each value) and describe your conversation:

1.

2.

3.

4.

5.

Parent Initials: _____

Describe a time or event with your teammates when you have made the decision to stand up for what you believe in? What happened? How was this choice a display of leadership?

List five things that you know and choose to be in complete control of when it comes to your own performance:

1.

2.

3.

4.

5.

The Big 'A' Word

Accountability is one of the most highly desired values in teams and includes self-discipline, personal responsibility, and conscious choices. Specifically, it is about your past choices, actions, and behaviors that have attributed to your results in the present.

So what does accountability in action look like when it comes to your current performance results? Here is a framework for practicing real accountability:

1. **Understand that all improvement starts with the truth.** What are the choices, actions, in-actions, decisions, assumptions, and behaviors that YOU made that have resulted in your current performance?

2. **Use accountability as a learning tool.** What can YOU learn that can help you get better moving forward? What do you need to continue? What needs to be changed? What's worth celebrating so far?

Instead of using accountability in a negative way as a punishment AFTER you have made a poor decision, **accountability is best used in the beginning of a season and should start with what you want and what you are willing to commit to.**

List 3 things that you are willing to be accountable for going in to the season?

1.

2.

3.

Accountability Partner Initials: _____

Describe below how you want to be held accountable when you slip up or fall behind? How do you want others to approach you? What do you want them to say?

The ESPN Interview

Pretend for a moment that you actually achieved your goals and desired results for this season and that ESPN is now doing a special interview with you about your athletic journey.

What does it feel like having achieved what you set out to accomplish?

What were some of your biggest roadblocks and obstacles along the way? How were you able to overcome them?

What do you think helped you to pull through, overcome your trials, and achieve your goals?

What advice would you have for other athletes out there watching, just like you, that want to be in your shoes?

Share your ESPN interview with your accountability partner and have them ask you the questions while you answer them out lout. Describe your conversation below:

Accountability Partner Initials: _____

Wrapping up, what is the one thing that you learned about yourself from this chapter that can have the greatest impact in your life and in your performance?

Becoming Great Is A Process

In steps eight, nine, and ten of this journal you have taken the time to really get to know yourself and choose yourself when it comes to your sport. You have also stepped up and had some critical conversations with your accountability partner, your coach, and your parents which serve only to help make you better.

The next step is now to take all of this information and start to develop yourself in becoming the best version of you that you want to be as an athlete and as a person.

Step #11: Swim Your Best
-Develop Yourself

"Make better decisions...get better results!"

Have you ever looked back once your season started and said to yourself '*If I had only spent more time doing X, than I would be performing so much better right now*?' This regretful thought could be about fitness, skill work, getting stronger, or even more flexible. And if this sounds like you, then it's really just about a choice you made at that time choosing to focus on something else. This step is about making yourself better and that starts with making good decisions and being intentional about the athlete that you want to be.

This can help or hurt your chances of getting better

If you want to get better and become your best then it's important that you develop good habits. What exactly is a habit? A habit is a consistent behavior that you do automatically without even consciously thinking about it. Habits help your brain conserve energy and put everyday routines and thoughts on auto-pilot. For example, biting your finger nails if you are nervous before a game is a habit, or even pumping your fist after you have made a great play is a habit.

However, not all habits actually help you! And it's like author John Maxwell says "we first form habits, then they form us."

One of the first things that I do when working with an athlete, is to have them identify their number one bad habit that is getting in the way of being able to swim their best.

So what about you? What habits have you developed that prevent you from swimming your best?

List your #1 bad habit below:

-

If you were to break this habit in the next thirty days, how would you be better as an athlete and as a person? What could you do differently?

I commit to being able to break my #1 bad habit in the next thirty days by replacing it with another one. My action plan for building this new habit each day is the following:

Your Initials:_____   Accountability Partner Initials: _____

Champions Know How To Leverage Their Routine Not Rely On It

Do you have a clear routine in place when it comes to preparing to perform your best? Routines give you a clear picture and solid foundation of what to expect in the weeks to come before a practice or before a big meet. Having this kind of clarity will help to give you more confidence in your performance as well as a competitive advantage over your competition.

Once you have your routine down and feel good about it, you can then make it a habit to where you don't even have to consciously think about what you are doing.

Rituals are just as important as routines except the main difference is the level of your intentional focus and attitude. For example, when you get up in the morning you probably have the same routine of getting out of bed, brushing your teeth, etc. which doesn't take a whole lot of thought. But then maybe on the day of your meet, you add the ritual of listening to your favorite song right when you wake up before you get going.

The following is a list of various items that go into planning your routines and rituals:

- season schedule of practice and games
- your favorite pre-meet meal the night before a big meet
- your morning routine the day of your meet when you wake up
- your favorite pre-meet music playlist that you like to listen to before every meet
- a specific warm-up routine to get you ready to swim your best
- a specific cool-down routine after practice and a meet
- a nutritional routine both pre and post competition and practice
- an active recovery routine during your off days to help re-energize your body

Other factors that go into creating your ideal rituals are positive self-talk, visualization, focus, and knowing how you want and need to feel (emotional control).

Use the space below to start to develop your own ideal rituals and routines that will help you consistently swim your best.

Favorite Pre-meet meal the night before your meet:

Favorite breakfast meal the day of your meet:

Favorite Pre-meet Music Playlist:

List your top three positive self-talk phrases that get you focused and in the mental state needed to swim your best (i.e. I trust my instincts or I am a good athlete and deserve to be here right now.):

1.

2.

3.

What happens when you make a mistake?

When an athlete makes a mistake, usually their self-talk turns negative and their body language completely changes to dropping their head, shrugging their shoulders, or get physically tense out of self-anger. For some athletes, they can't let go of a mistake even ten minutes after it has already occurred! Why? Either they are putting way too much pressure on themselves to perform, or they are scared how their coach might react if they perform poorly. Both reasons will only serve to prevent you from swimming your best, so don't let this happen to you.

First of all, realize that there is no such thing as a perfect race or performance and that everyone makes mistakes. It's what you choose to do with your mistakes after you make them that matters most. This is where having a mistake ritual can help to keep you focused on being present during the race instead of carrying around frustration.

A mistake ritual is a process to help you deal with your mistake, learn from it, and then get refocused back in the meet. There are a number of different kinds of mistake rituals such as specific self-talk phrases, acting like you are physically throwing the mistake away, pinching yourself, etc.

A simple mistake ritual can even be something like the following:

1. What were you trying to do?
2. What went wrong?
3. If given the chance to do it over again what would you do differently?
4. Move on to the next event

Describe your own mistake ritual below:

Now share it with your accountability partner. Describe your conversation below:

Accountability Partner Initials: _____

Fueling for Performance...It Definitely Matters

Your nutritional habits play a huge part in your ability to consistently swim your best. The what-when-where-why-how of sports nutrition can be the difference between whether or not you achieve your desired results.

Although there simply isn't enough room in this journal to discuss in detail sports nutrition principles, there is one thing that MUST be mentioned. In fact, it is usually the #1 most ignored part of good nutritional habits of athletes. Can you guess what it is?

If you're an athlete, you MUST eat breakfast every day!

However Sugar Smacks and Honey Comb Cereal don't count. And neither does having just a protein shake. Instead try eggs, a bagel with peanut butter, yogurt, fruit, etc. You can't expect to have energy for an intense workout or game if you don't eat breakfast.

Write down your favorite breakfast foods below:

For a great resource of what the best athletes use for sports nutrition choices visit www.athletebydesign.com/nutrition

Meet with your parents about how they can best help to hold you accountable for eating a good breakfast. It might even mean you have to start waking up five minutes extra early!

Parent Initials: _____

What Happens When Decision Making Gets Difficult?

Making good decisions isn't always easy, but it is easier when you know what's contributing to your poor decision making. Therefore, use the following 5 D's as a litmus test for making great decisions!

1. **Distractions (both positive and negative)**
2. **Distortions (lack of clarity and understanding)**
3. **Discouragement (personal attacks and sarcasm)**
4. **Disengagement (lack of interest)**
5. **Dissonance (your actions and words don't align)**

Which of the 5 D's of Decision Making do you struggle with the most? Why?

What needs to happen in order overcome it?

Share your results with your accountability partner and describe your conversation below:

Accountability Partner Initials: _____

If You Want To Consistently Swim Your Best

What if you were able to repeat your best performance every time you swim? Is this even possible? I wish! But it is possible to consistently give your best. In order to do so, you must first identify some of your best performances and think through all of the underlying factors that might have contributed to doing so.

Describe your top three best performances in the past year. What factors can you identify that contributed to you being able to play your best? How many of these factors are in your control? How can you make these repeatable?

1.

2.

3.

Wrapping up, what is the one thing that you learned about yourself from this chapter that can have the greatest impact in your life and in your performance?

Now that you have worked through some of the key issues of developing yourself and doing what it takes to become your best, I want to introduce you to the Energy Management Tracker Worksheet. It is a self-management tool designed to help you better understand how your energy is affecting your performance. It takes less than two minutes to complete at the end of each day and I think you will find it just as useful as the rest of the athletes who have participated in Athlete By Design™ programs.

Energy Management Tracker Worksheet

How many times have you tried to get psyched up for a big event only to start off mediocre at best? Even worse, your coach starts yelling at you to get focused and ready to go but you still struggle to do so?

*FACT: You are only as good as your body's
ability to recover*

The following worksheet is designed for you to better manage your daily energy. The world's greatest champions make time to know themselves and their own bodies. Accountability to yourself has to come first if you want to be the athlete that you want to be!

Directions
On the following pages you will notice there are seven different categories to answer, some objective and some subjective in nature. All you will need to do is put a dot next to the correct choice for each category for that day.

You will then total up the number of points in the column and place your sum score at the bottom of the page to give you a *Daily Points score*. Below is the scoring key for your reference:

28-35 points: Gold
20-27points: Silver
12-19 points: Bronze

If your score is Gold or Silver than you are doing a good job of energy management and are giving yourself the best chance to compete. However, if your score is a Bronze, you should be concerned about your ability to perform and possible even postpone training if possible.

It's All About You
Remember, you are the head of 'Team You'! In order to swim your best more often it is important to develop energy management skills. This worksheet will last the entire month and there are a total of three months for you.

Month: _____

EMT SCORECARD

*KEY: (35-29 Points)-**Starter** (28-22 Points)-**Back up** (21-15Points)-**Third String** (14-8 Points)-**Benchwarmer** (7-0 Points)-**Stay at Home***

Points	Water Intake	1	2	3	4	5	6	7	8	9	10	11	12	13	14	15	16	17	18	19	20	21	22	23	24	25	26	27	28	29	30	31
5	10 Glasses																															
4	8 Glasses																															
3	6 Glasses																															
2	4 Glasses																															
1	2 Glasses																															

	Meals per Day																															
5	6																															
4	5																															
3	4																															
2	3																															
1	2																															

	Hours of Sleep																															
5	8																															
4	7																															
3	6																															
2	5																															
1	4																															

Tiredness Sensation

5	Very Rested																																			
4	Normal																																			
3	Tired																																			
2	Very Tired																																			
1	Dog Tired																																			

Training Willingness

5	Let's Go!																																			
4	Good																																			
3	Poor																																			
2	Unwilling																																			
1	Did Not Train																																			

Appetite

5	Very Good																																			
4	Good																																			
3	Poor																																			
2	Very Poor																																			
1	Did Not Eat																																			

Competitive Willingness

5	High																																			
4	Average																																			
3	Low																																			
2	Not At All																																			
2	TOTAL DAILY POINTS																																			

Month: _____

EMT SCORECARD

KEY *(35-29 Points)*-**Starter** *(28-22 Points)*-**Back up** *(21-15Points)*-**Third String** *(14-8 Points)*-**Benchwarmer** *(7-0 Points)*-**Stay at Home**

Points	Water Intake	1	2	3	4	5	6	7	8	9	10	11	12	13	14	15	16	17	18	19	20	21	22	23	24	25	26	27	28	29	30	31
5	10 Glasses																															
4	8 Glasses																															
3	6 Glasses																															
2	4 Glasses																															
1	2 Glasses																															

	Meals per Day
5	6
4	5
3	4
2	3
1	2

	Hours of Sleep
5	8
4	7
3	6
2	5
1	4

Tiredness Sensation

5	Very Rested
4	Normal
3	Tired
2	Very Tired
1	Dog Tired

Training Willingness

5	Let's Go!
4	Good
3	Poor
2	Unwilling
1	Did Not Train

Appetite

5	Very Good
4	Good
3	Poor
2	Very Poor
1	Did Not Eat

Competitive Willingness

5	High
4	Average
3	Low
2	Not At All
	TOTAL DAILY POINTS

Month: _____

EMT SCORECARD

KEY: (35-29 Points)-*Starter* (28-22 Points)-*Back up* (21-15Points)-*Third String* (14-8 Points)-*Benchwarmer* (7-0 Points)-*Stay at Home*

Points	Water Intake	1	2	3	4	5	6	7	8	9	10	11	12	13	14	15	16	17	18	19	20	21	22	23	24	25	26	27	28	29	30	31
5	10 Glasses																															
4	8 Glasses																															
3	6 Glasses																															
2	4 Glasses																															
1	2 Glasses																															

	Meals per Day																															
5	6																															
4	5																															
3	4																															
2	3																															
1	2																															

	Hours of Sleep																															
5	8																															
4	7																															
3	6																															
2	5																															
1	4																															

Tiredness Sensation

5	Very Rested
4	Normal
3	Tired
2	Very Tired
1	Dog Tired

Training Willingness

5	Let's Go!
4	Good
3	Poor
2	Unwilling
1	Did Not Train

Appetite

5	Very Good
4	Good
3	Poor
2	Very Poor
1	Did Not Eat

Competitive Willingness

5	High
4	Average
3	Low
2	Not At All

TOTAL DAILY POINTS

Step #12: You Did It
-Celebrate

"The more you praise and celebrate your life, the more you have to celebrate." -Oprah Winfrey

What you celebrate matters! As you have learned throughout this journal, celebration isn't always just about the outcome of your performance. It is so much more than that!

This is the fun step! Now you get to look back at your journey and celebrate all of the hard work that you put in to become the best version of you!   Did you achieve your desired results? Was it worth all of the time and effort? Most of all was it fun?

Below is the **Best Version Of You Inventory** to help you celebrate your accomplishments:

What was your most positive memorable moment? Why?

In what ways are you different than you were when you first started?

Looking back over these last few weeks, what did you learn most about yourself?

What are you most proud of and what is worthy of a huge celebration?

What were some of the things that you accomplished that make you appreciate yourself more?

What were your top three most special moments?

What are the top three things that you learned that made you a better swimmer?

What are your top three life lessons that you learned?

How did your relationship with your parents, teammates, and coach change throughout this journal?

Parents:

Teammates/Accountability Partner:

Coach:

Describe in a few paragraphs how the best version of you transformed during these twelve steps:

Hang On...You're Not Done Yet

There are a few things left to do to wrap up. Here is a simple checklist for you to follow as you get ready to enjoy your offseason or transition into your next season!

- ☐ Schedule time in the immediate future to share what all you have written down with your parents, your accountability partner, and your coach

- ☐ Be sure and thank your parents for all of their support during your competitive season. Tell them three specific examples of how they best supported you.

- ☐ Thank your coach and tell him/her three different examples of how s/he helped you to become a better swimmer and person

- ☐ What will be your big 3 (things that you want to achieve) in your next upcoming season?

- ☐ Thank your accountability partner for holding you accountable and helping you to become the best version of you as an athlete that you want to be.

Spend some time celebrating and acknowledging all of your hard work and achievements. But be sure and recognize that this is only a chapter in your story of your athletic journey. As you start the next chapter, I would encourage you to look back at the beginning of this journal and let it serve as a resource and reminder for what it takes for you to be your best!

Thanks again for letting me be a part of your team,

J. Boone

Use the Swim Your Best Journal™ During Your Next Season

If you just finished your short course season while working through this journal, start back over as you begin your long course season as your mindset changes as you get better and gain more experience.

Order additional copies of the Swim Your Best Journal™ for each of your competitive short course and long course seasons by visiting www.athletebydesign.com.

Contact us at athletebydesign@gmail.com to find out about team discounts.

Master Your Mental Game

Do you physically dominate your competition but always wind up just short of a win due to lack of concentration or a dumb mental mistake? There is little arguement that an athlete's mental game is what is most important on gameday. However, getting mentally ready to play your best can often be challenging for many athletes, especially on a day to day basis.

Take the Ready To Play Mental Profile™ and discover EXACTLY what you need to do to improve your mental performance. Used by athletes all over the world, this online assessment will reveal your current mental capacity in the top ten mental areas of athletic success. (includes a workbook)

Visit http://www.athletebydesign.com/ for more information.

103

Parent Your Best™

Every parent wants the best for their child when it comes to sports. However, today's youth sports culture is having a negative impact on Sports Parents with even the best of intentions for their child. In *Parent Your Best*, author Jeremy Boone goes beyond the traditional Sports Psychology approach to parenting and gives you a blueprint that shows you HOW to be the reason your child succeeds in sport. Your child has a coach to teach them skills in their sport, and this book will serve as your own personal coach in your efforts to parent your best.

Visit www.parentyourbest.com for more information.

Coach Your Best™

In this ground breaking new book, international performance coach Jeremy Boone shares a unique approach to coaching based on Sports Axiology, the science of human value and decision making in sports. In it you will find a simple framework for creating a winning culture and a practical approach for maximizing your athlete's potential no matter what sport they play.

Visit www.coachyourbest.com for more information.

*For more swimming resources visit www.athletebydesign.com/swimming

ABOUT THE AUTHOR

 Jeremy Boone is the founder of Athlete By Design in Charlotte, NC, and is an internationally recognized performance coach, speaker, author, researcher, and consultant. During his fifteen years of coaching he has had the fortunate opportunity to work with players and teams in multiple sports in five countries including the opportunity to be a part of the NFL Carolina Panthers Offseason Program for seven years serving as the speed & conditioning coach. His main areas of focus in the past have been ACL Injury Prevention and sport-specific speed development. For more about Jeremy visit **www.athletebydesign.com**

He is also considered one of the world's leading authorities in Sports Axiology, the science of human value in sport. Using this science, he has co-developed mental profiles for coaches and athletes of all sports used to determine an individual's unique decision making pattern based on their value system. These results help take the guesswork out of designing customized mental performance strategies to help athletes and coaches perform their best. For more information about Sports Axiology visit **www.sportsaxiology.com**.

17761660R00056

Made in the USA
Charleston, SC
27 February 2013